ADVENTURES IN FRONTIER AMERICA

FRONTIER DREAM

Life on the Great Plains

by Catherine E. Chambers

Illustrated by Dick Smolinski

Troll Associates

Library of Congress Cataloging in Publication Data

Chambers, Catherine E.
    Frontier dream.

    (Adventures in frontier America)
    Summary: A Norwegian family suffers great hardship as
they try to establish a farm on the plains of the Dakota
territory in the 1870's.
    [1. Frontier and pioneer life—Great Plains—Fiction.
2. Great Plains—Fiction]   I. Smolinski, Dick, ill.
II. Title.   III. Series: Chambers, Catherine E.
Adventures in frontier America.
PZ7.C3558Fr   1984   [Fic]   83-18282
ISBN 0-8167-0039-7 (lib. bdg.)
ISBN 0-8167-0040-0 (pbk.)

FRONTIER DREAM

Life on the Great Plains

Twelve-year-old Katrin Isaacsen couldn't believe her ears. Pa was talking about moving again, and Mama had just had a baby a month ago. Worse, he had already filed for land—in the western plains of Dakota Territory! "Wasn't life in Omaha hard enough?" thought Katrin.

Pa saw the look on Mama's face. "I'll go first," he said. "I'll build a shelter and get things started. You and the children can come in summer, when the baby's bigger." He didn't say how they were all to manage while he was gone. Pa was like that, a dreamer. He had to be, Mama had told Katrin more than once. Otherwise he never would have brought her here from Norway when they married. In America there was a future, Pa often said. Back in Norway he could never have hoped to own a farm. Katrin sometimes thought life in Norway couldn't possibly be any worse than here.

5

In Omaha, the Isaacsens lived in a one-room cabin that was only a shack. It was the best Pa could do on their most recent move. They had been leapfrogging all over the West as long as Katrin could remember. If only they could settle down, like the Olsens who kept the boarding house down the street! That was what Pa did mean to do now, didn't he? Katrin wished she could believe him. Pa's blue eyes grew hurt when the rest of the family didn't share in his excitement. "It's time the little ones were in bed. We'll talk tomorrow," Mama said quietly.

Dagmar, who was sixteen, stood up and reached for her shawl. "I'm going to visit the Olsens," she said. Dagmar loved the Olsens' big frame house with its pretty furniture. Mrs. Olsen, a widow, was like a kind aunt to the Isaacsens, and to her boarders, as well. Katrin hoped Mrs. Olsen could make Dagmar feel better, but she doubted it. Dagmar and Lars Olsen had been keeping company these past three months, and Dagmar wasn't going to want to leave him.

6

The next night, Dagmar didn't come to the supper table. Later, when Katrin and Mama were washing dishes in the tin washtub, she and Lars came in. Their faces were pale.

"Pa," Dagmar said. "Mama. Please, I want you to listen to what Lars has to say."

Lars twisted his hat in his hands, but his voice was firm. "Mr. Isaacsen, Dagmar and I love each other. We want your permission to get married. Dagmar doesn't want to go with you to the prairie. And something more— my mother and I would like to have Mrs. Isaacsen and the young ones stay at the boarding house till you get a house built on your land. In exchange, Mrs. Isaacsen could help my mother cook for the boarders."

Pa didn't like the idea of a wedding so soon, but he agreed. Dagmar was a grown woman. If they married right away he could attend the ceremony. He was glad to think of his family staying with the Olsens. That eased his conscience a bit about leaving them behind.

Soon the little household was broken up. Once again Mama packed her dishes and her few precious possessions in barrels. They were put away in the Olsens' cellar. Mama, Katrin, eight-year-old Nels, and baby Eric shared a big room in the Olsen house. "We must try to help Mrs. Olsen all we can," Mama said. "She is being very kind."

So Mama cooked many good meals for the boarding-house table. Katrin dusted and ironed and washed dishes. Dagmar helped Mrs. Olsen with housekeeping. Even Nels ran errands and split firewood under Lars' friendly guidance. Pa had gone out to his claim, taking a bedroll, the family horse, and a rickety wagon.

Spring came slowly on the Great Plains. First, the ice broke on the stream. Then the earth thawed, inch by inch. At last, wildflowers began poking up amid the prairie grasses.

Mama got a letter, brought by the post rider. "Pa's ready for us to come," she told them.

Mrs. Olsen lent them money to go by train. This was an adventure, jolting north across the plains at the amazing speed of eleven miles an hour! The train pulled to a stop in the middle of nowhere, and there was Pa waiting with Old Gray and the wagon. It was newly painted blue, with red flowers and green leaves—just like the special tray Mama had brought from Norway! Pa was beaming, he was so glad to see them. He couldn't get over how baby Eric had grown in the past three months.

Mama was smiling, too. But she stopped smiling when they reached Pa's land. "Chris Isaacsen! You didn't tell me all you had for us was a tent!"

'Now, Sigrid, this will be fine for summer! The air's clean as paradise, and it's warm. It will do the children good to sleep out."

10

Little Nels was delighted. And it was beautiful here in the flowering grasses. Only there were no trees and no houses, as far as the eye could see!

If Mr. Isaacsen lived for five years on this barren land, he could have it for free. In the early days of the westward movement, *all* land had been free. Anyone who wanted it just came and settled on it. Now, all unclaimed land east of Indian territory belonged to the United States government. Settlers bought land, usually at two dollars an acre, from government land offices. Settlers who had no money were called squatters, for they just claimed the land and lived on it as if it were their own. If new owners showed up, or army troops came to drive them off, they moved on.

12

These were the years of the Great Migration, the time when pioneers moved westward to settle America's frontier. In the beginning, some families settled through the woodlands west to the Mississippi River, while others went far beyond it—beyond the prairies and plains, beyond the Rockies, to Oregon or California. Most farmers believed that in the Great Plains, where trees didn't grow, crops would not grow either, so they did not settle there.

Things changed after railroads were built across the country, stretching all the way to California. Both the government and the railroad companies wanted American settlers on the Great Plains. Settlements and towns would help protect the railroads from Indian attacks. In 1862, Congress passed the Homestead Act. It said that anyone who staked a claim and lived on it for five years became a landowner without paying a cent. The railroads also bought large tracts of land and offered it free to people who would come and settle. They hoped to make money in the future by transporting people and freight back and forth between homesteads and towns.

The railroad companies also spread the news of free land to the people of Europe. They asked farmers to come to the American frontier. People from all over Europe came to the "land of opportunity." Poor families crossed the Atlantic in the steerage, or lower deck, of a steamship. They slept on hard boards. They had to bring their own food, and they took turns cooking on dangerous stoves. Sometimes children came alone. Many people died before they reached America. Some immigrants stayed in seaport cities like Boston and New York. But many farmers went west to the frontier. Usually, they had no money. What they had was a willingness to work, and a dream. That is how Chris and Sigrid Isaacsen came to Omaha. Pa had worked at any jobs he could get. Now he wanted his own land. He knew he could be a good farmer once his crops were planted.

15

steel plow

Mr. Isaacsen didn't know what the land of the Great Plains would be like. He found that the soil was rich and good for growing. But there were no trees, and there was very little rain. The buffalo grass grew so thick that iron plows and shovels would not cut through it. A farmer needed one of the new steel plows. Without a sharp steel blade he could not plant a field. He needed to dig a well at least a hundred feet deep. To do that he needed a springpole drilling rig with a steel "bit" at the end of a long iron pole.

A farmer with money could hire a steam rig to dig his well. He could pay quarrymen to bring him stone for a house. He could pay for the wood for furniture and fences.

He could have a McCormick reaper that harvested his wheat, and a threshing machine pulled by five teams of horses. But most of the men who came to the Great Plains had to depend on their own labor. Often they worked for wealthier farmers. In exchange, they could borrow the farmer's plow to work their own land. This is what Chris Isaacsen did. All day, under the fierce sun, he worked for Mr. Worth. All day, Mama and Katrin tried to clear a garden patch with an ax. Nels and Katrin gathered dried grass for fuel.

One day, several bundles of dry grass caught fire while Mama and Katrin were far out on the prairie. Nels was alone watching the baby. Using a blanket, Nels smothered the fire. There was no other way to put it out, for they had no well. Every afternoon Pa brought a barrel of water the three miles home from the Worth place.

"We *must* have a well *soon*," Mama cried.

"We can't till harvest," Pa answered. "Then a drill is coming to the Worth spread. Mr. Worth will let us use it. What we must do *now* is build a shelter for the animals."

Every day after Pa came home, he cut some blocks of grass-covered earth called sod. For sod was what many barns and houses of the Great Plains were built of. Everyone except baby Eric helped. They built a small three-sided barn. The roof was also made of sod. Wildflowers bloomed on it and looked very pretty.

One afternoon when Pa came home, he found Katrin and little Eric playing on the roof. He yanked them down. *"Don't you ever go up there again!* The roof could cave in under you!"

Pa took Nels to help Mr. Worth with the harvesting. Mama and Katrin helped Mrs. Worth cook for all the extra farm hands Mr. Worth hired. Mrs. Worth paid Katrin fifty cents for her work.

After the harvest, the well drill came to the Worths' farm. Pa and Nels helped then, too. Afterwards the drill and the other homesteaders came to the Isaacsen spread. The drill hung from a long pole, and men worked it by jigging up and down with their feet in stirrups. Like everything else on the prairie, this was a long backbreaking job. The well they drilled was a hundred and seventy-eight feet deep.

"You're lucky at that," Mr. Worth told Pa. "Sometimes the water lies as much as three hundred feet underground."

Pa wiped his forehead with his kerchief and didn't say anything.

By summer's end all the Isaacsens were browned and blistered. Katrin had calluses on her hands and feet. Soon chill winds whipped across the plains. Rain dripped into the tent and lay in puddles on the floor.

"I am taking the children back to Omaha," Mama told
Pa. "Mrs. Olsen will give me work. If you must stay here
through the winter, you must. But the children are going
to be warm and dry. We will try to earn money to help."

"I'll put the tent across the front of the stable," Pa said.
"The animals will keep me warm. We have our well now.
By next summer things will be fine."

"Next summer," Mama said clearly, "we must have a house. Otherwise the children and I will not come back."

Katrin almost hated Mama for saying that. She almost hated herself for being glad to get back to Mrs. Olsen's comfortable house. Pa stood by the railroad tracks and waved good-bye as their train pulled away. He looked very small against the endless plains.

That winter Mama made pickles to sell. After school, Katrin did laundry for Mrs. Olsen's boarders. Nels ran errands.

The coins piled up slowly in Mama's blue coffeepot.

In March Pa had been homesteading for a whole year on his claim. In May he wrote to Mama, "You and the children can plan to come."

That meant a house. It must!

On the day they were to go to the homestead, Dagmar was sick. Mama was troubled. "I can't leave your sister. There is no way to let Pa know in time. Katrin, you and Nels must go alone. Tell Pa that Eric and I will come soon."

It was exciting to ride on the train alone. It was exciting to count the money they had earned, and think how proud Pa would be. But when the train stopped, Pa wasn't there. Old Gray and the wagon weren't there. Nothing but wind and prairie, as far as eyes could see. The train disappeared across the plains with a lonely whistle.

Katrin and Nels looked at each other. Without a word they started through the waving sea of grass. They knew from the sun which way Pa's land lay. Soon they found the trail that wagon wheels had worn across the prairie. They walked and walked. They took their shoes off and walked some more.

"Katrin, I'm scared," Nels said. Katrin nodded. Only
something bad could have kept Pa away. At last they
came over a rise and saw the homestead below them in the
hollow. The open-side barn had been turned into a tiny
house. Everything was so still. The plow lay by itself in the
middle of a furrow. Old Gray whinnied mournfully and
nuzzled them with a dry nose. Her water trough was
empty. *Where was Pa?*

"Katrin, I hear something," Nels whispered. Katrin
didn't answer. She was pushing aside the canvas doorflap.
At first she couldn't see well in the darkness.

A crude bed stood in one corner. On it was a pile of
blankets. A faint moaning came from them.

"*Pa!*" Katrin ran to him. Pa was doubled up, clutching his side. His head was burning hot, but he shook with chill. He didn't know them! His eyes stared at Katrin without seeing her, and he mumbled in Norwegian.

"We have to get help." Katrin swung round to Nels. "Stay by him. Pump some water and sponge his face. I'm going to find a doctor!"

Were there any doctors on the prairie? She didn't know. She untied the horse and quickly gave her water. Then she flung herself on, bareback. The Worth place was closest. They would know what to do. She galloped away, finding her way by the sinking sun.

Mr. Worth and another man were plowing in the fields. One of the men caught Old Gray's bridle as Katrin slid down, sobbing. "Pa...he's very sick. He needs a doctor."

Then Katrin was in the house, and Mrs. Worth was giving her a cool drink. Mr. Worth was having his best horse saddled. "I'll find Doc Simpson at Thorsens' Junction. I'll send a telegram for your Mama to come, Katrin. You and my wife go back to your Pa."

Katrin and Mrs. Worth rode through the twilight as fast as the Worths' wagon could carry them.

Pa was worse. Katrin knew that right away. She and Mrs. Worth bathed him and tried to make him comfortable. Hours later, Mr. Worth and the doctor arrived. The doctor's face was somber as he examined Pa by lantern light.

"Appendicitis. We'll have to operate right away."

They brought the side boards from the wagon in and laid them across barrels to make a table. Mr. Worth and the doctor lifted Pa onto it. They stood lanterns at each corner, and Mr. Worth and Nels held lanterns on either side. Mrs. Worth gave Pa chloroform. Katrin had to help the doctor. It seemed like hours before the operation was over.

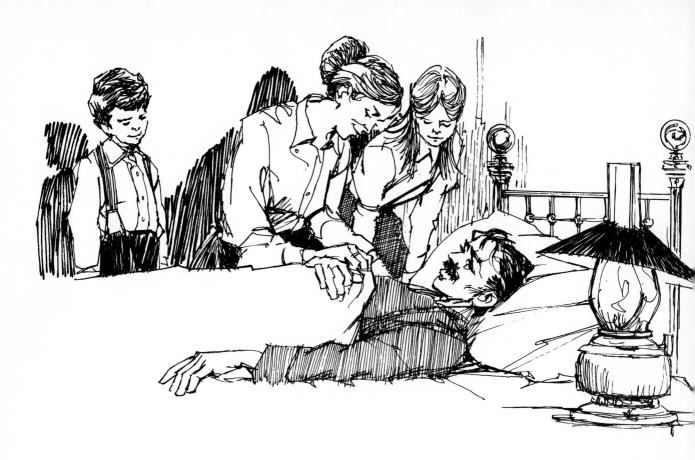

"We got it out in time. His fever will go down now,"
the doctor said. "He'll need nursing."

"I'll stay to help Katrin with it," Mrs. Worth said. "We
can move Mr. Isaacsen to our house when he's better."

The next day Pa's fever broke. Now he knew who Nels
and Katrin were. In a few days they moved him to the
Worths' farm. He was much better, but still very weak.
Mama was there, with little Eric and happy news. Dagmar
and Lars had a baby boy!

"Another Viking," Pa murmured. "He'll have to go far to live up to his aunt and uncle." He was very proud of all Katrin and Nels had done.

News of Pa's sickness traveled quickly across the prairie. While he was still at the Worths', men brought horses and plows and furrowed his land. They cut three-foot blocks of sod to build a bigger "soddy," as the sod houses were called. "On the frontier, folks have to help each other," Mr. Worth said when Pa tried to thank him.

All summer Katrin and Nels worked in the fields. Mama worked there with little Eric beside her. They raised their first crop of wheat. With the money Mama and the children had made in Omaha, Pa was able to buy tools. He bought wood for rafters for the sod house. In August, Dagmar and Lars and the baby came to visit. They helped with the harvest. Lars would take the wheat back to Omaha and sell it.

After harvest came the house-raising. Again, the neighbors came to help. They built a sod house with walls three feet thick. The back of the house was dug into a rise of ground. There was a window on each side of the house, and two in front. Katrin was proud that her money had helped buy the glass. The door was wood and faced away from the worst winds. Now the little house could be a barn again.

The Isaacsen furniture and household things came by train from Omaha. Mama's painted chairs again stood around the big heavy table. Her pretty Norwegian tray was on the mantel. That winter, the family stayed together at the homestead.

The sod house was cool in summer and warm in winter. When the snows thawed, the roof leaked. Mama had to hold an umbrella over her while she turned flapjacks at the iron stove. Rain sometimes dripped on the children when they slept. But most times it was cozy being a family again, sitting together around the fire while snow blanketed the plains.

By the next winter, they had a buffalo-skin rug to keep their feet warm. They slept under buffalo skins, too. Now Nels was old enough to be a real help in the fields. Katrin was earning money doing laundry for the field hands who worked for Mr. Worth. She was thinking of starting a school. It was time for Eric to learn his ABC's.

Pa's farm was doing well. When the five years of homesteading were up, Pa drove to the government land office, and all the family went with him. Mr. Worth and another neighbor also went—to witness that the Isaacsens had worked and lived on their homestead for five full years. Pa paid his registration fee and signed and dated the deed. It was March 13, 1876. This was the first time, as far back as anyone could remember, that Isaacsens had owned their own land.

"In America, all things are possible," Pa said, smiling.

"In America, everything really *is* possible," Katrin thought. "If you work hard and have faith. And if you have a family like ours."

She was very proud to be an Isaacsen—and a pioneer!